The Power of Being a Woman Devotional

Embracing the Triumph of the Feminine Spirit

Michelle McKinney Hammond

Published by MMH Ministries

Print ISBN: 978-1-7360427-3-1

Ebook ISBN: 978-1-7360427-2-4

Copyright © 2021 by Michelle McKinney Hammond. All rights reserved.

Formatted for Publication by Ben Wolf

www.benwolf.com/editing-services/

Photography by DexDee Photography

Cover Design by Tega Baah

Verses marked NIV are taken from the Holy Bible, New International Version®. NIV®. Copyright © 1973, 1978, 1984 by the International Bible Society. Used by permission of Zondervan. All rights reserved.

Verses marked KJV are taken from the King James Version of the Bible.

Verses marked NKJV are taken from the New King James Version. Copyright © 1982 by Thomas Nelson, Inc. Used by permission.

Verses marked NLT are taken from the *Holy Bible,* New Living Translation, copyright © 1996. Used by permission of Tyndale House Publishers, Inc., Wheaton, IL 60189. All rights reserved.

Verses marked AMP are taken from The Amplified Bible, Copyright © 1954, 1958, 1962, 1964, 1965, 1987 by The Lockman Foundation. All rights reserved. Used by permission.

Verses marked NEB are taken from The New English Bible, copyright © Oxford University Press and Cambridge University Press 1961, 1970. All rights reserved.

Verses marked TLB are taken from *The Living Bible,* Copyright © 1971. Used by permission of Tyndale House Publishers, Inc., Wheaton, IL 60189 USA. All rights reserved.

Verses marked NASB are taken from the New American Standard Bible®, © 1960, 1962, 1963, 1968, 1971, 1972, 1973, 1975, 1977, 1995 by The Lockman Foundation. Used by permission. (www.Lockman.org)

A NOTE FROM THE AUTHOR

WELCOME MY SISTER,

WELCOME TO THE JOURNEY BACK TO YOU! BACK TO THE GARDEN. BACK TO GOD'S ORIGINAL INTENTION OF WHO YOU WERE DESIGNED TO BE.

---MICHELLE MCKINNEY HAMMOND

MICHELLEHAMMOND.COM

YOU MAY HAVE CONFLICTING VIEWS ON THIS THING CALLED "WOMANHOOD" AND "FEMININITY" BUT TRUST ME, IT IS A DIVINE GIFT FROM ABOVE THAT IS SURE TO ENHANCE THE QUALITY OF YOUR LIFE AND THOSE WHO SURROUND YOU WHEN YOU EMBRACE AND CELEBRATE ALL THAT IT ENTAILS.

CONTRARY TO WHAT SOCIETY PROJECTS WOMEN WERE CREATED TO BE UNIQUE, MASTERFUL, POWERFUL AND A VALUABLE ASSET TO THE WORLD AT LARGE. THE ENEMY OF OUR SOULS SEEKS TO PERVERT GOD'S ORIGINAL DESIGN BECAUSE HE KNOWS THE THREAT YOU CAUSE TO HIS DEVICES AND PLAN.

AH, BUT GOD IS GREATER, AND HIS PURPOSES PREVAIL ABOVE ALL OTHER CONSPIRACIES AND MANIPULATIONS. WOMEN ARE OVERCOMERS! FLOURISHING AND RISING IN THE FACE OF SEEMINGLY CONFOUNDING ODDS AND CHALLENGES. THAT CAN BE YOU!!!

THE SECRET TO OVERCOMING IS FOUND IN BEING YOUR AUTHENTIC SELF. WALKING IN ALIGNMENT WITH GOD'S DESIGN RELEASES YOU TO LIVE TO YOUR ULTIMATE POTENTIAL. THIS IS WHERE YOU NO LONGER PURSUE VICTORY IN YOUR LIFE BECAUSE VICTORY IS PURSUING YOU!!!!

ARE YOU READY TO BE YOUR ULTIMATE MOST POWERFUL SELF? LET'S TAKE THIS JOURNEY TOGETHER!

Michelle McKinney Hammond

Michelle McKinney Hammond
MMH (Me, Myself & Him) Ministries

WOMAN TO WOMAN

MICHELLEHAMMOND.COM | © 2020 THE POWER OF BEING A WOMAN

CHAPTER ONE

WOMAN TO WOMAN

GOD CREATED HUMANITY IN GOD'S OWN IMAGE, IN THE DIVINE IMAGE GOD CREATED THEM, MALE AND FEMALE GOD CREATED THEM. GENESIS 1:27, CEB

Somewhere between her home
and a placard demanding equal rights
she got lost
wandering past the garden
following where the serpent pointed
she turned left instead of right and got off track
...and though the scenery looked vaguely familiar
a frown of consternation
began to crease her brow
as she realized
it was taking her
far too long
to reach her desired destination
still she determined to go
yet another mile
before turning off her chosen path
perhaps she was being too anxious...
and as she wandered
looking for a marker to get her bearings
man wondered where she'd gone
as she ventured too far to hear his need for her
or her children crying
and they too lost their way trying to follow her
misled by traces of her perfume in the air
the memory of a gentle touch
an encouraging word...
a piece of fabric soft to the skin
and sage advice
were found along the path
now littered with confusion and distrust...
and as man's shoulders began to slope in resignation
weakening his arms
causing him to abdicate his seat as protector
and her children began to find their own way
allowing new friends of rebellion
to fill the space she left behind
a cry rang out...
it filled the earth
it reached the skies
and rang throughout the heavens

MICHELLEHAMMOND.COM |

"Woman, where art thou?"
"Woman, where art thou?"
"Woman, where art thou?"
it echoed off the mountaintops
and stretched across the plains
it descended throughout the valleys
this plaintive cry
mourning the absence
of this precious lost treasure
and she hearing the cry
came to a halt
not quite sure of where she stood
unable to give her location she turned
looking for her own footprints in the sand
only to find shallow remembrances of where she had been
and somewhere between her struggle to recall her true identity
and the place of her restoration
she saw visions of a man with sad eyes
longing for her love praying for her return
and children with their arms outstretched
crying for her wisdom to save them
but she had grown weary from the journey...
sadness rooting her to the spot
depression bowing her
into herself
she succumbed to her fatigue
sinking into a deep and fitful sleep...
and in the distance
the ring of hammers
began hesitantly
building
and building again
until it reverberated
through the land ...
its sharp rhythm piercing the hearts of men
awakening sleeping women
and frustrated children
as wanted signs were posted
by determined hands
in search of the vanishing woman...

> It's in Christ that we find out who we are and what we are living for. Long before we first heard of Christ and got our hopes up, he had his eye on us, had designs on us for glorious living, part of the overall purpose he is working out in everything and everyone. — Ephesians 1:11-12, MSG

Who are you? Who are you really? Amidst the layers of all the commitments we make and the voices that tug on us from every direction it becomes difficult to locate yourself. Our identity becomes murky smothered by the expectations of others, the projections we continually witness on social media and other visual outlets. The influence of the world creates an uncomfortable tension between the flesh and the spirit. We are, after all, spiritual beings having a natural experience.

Like the characters in "Third Rock From the Sun", aliens who found themselves assigned to live on earth, we find ourselves mystified by the habits of "earthlings." People in the world have no heavenly vision or understanding, which sets the stage for literally having to make up life as you go. Devoid of a set standard, many find themselves drifting from one ideology to another. Ethics and morals have shifted drastically over time because there is nothing to measure any set of beliefs by. But for those of us who know God intimately we know that our identity is hidden in the One who gave His life for us—Christ Jesus. He becomes the blueprint of our identity as well as how we are to walk out our everyday life. He is the one who reveals to us who we truly are and what we are living for. While the world has a lot to say about women that may attack our self-esteem.

God sees women as priceless treasures! God is fiercely passionate and protective of His women. It is the enemy's intention to make women feel discarded and devalued because he is aware of the power of a woman. Make no mistake a woman in alignment with her God is a force to be reckoned with!

PONDER THIS

1. How do you feel about being a woman?

2. In what ways do you feel short-changed or diminished? In what ways do you feel empowered?

3. Write a confession about your power as a woman and how you intend to proceed from here.

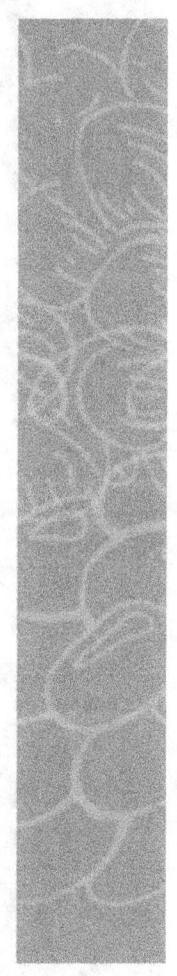

MICHELLEHAMMOND.COM |

LET'S PRAY

Dear Heavenly Father, there are so many voices with various expectations filling my world. Sometimes I find myself confused and even frustrated in my search to establish who I really am. Help me to remember that You hold the key to my true identity. As I seek you, I find myself and the purpose for which I was created. I will embrace and celebrate my divine identity and cast off all other voices that contradict your Word, in Jesus' name. Amen.

MICHELLEHAMMOND.COM |

BACK TO BASICS

MICHELLEHAMMOND.COM | © 2020 THE POWER OF BEING A WOMAN

CHAPTER TWO

BACK TO BASICS

THEN THE LORD GOD MADE A WOMAN FROM THE RIB, AND HE BROUGHT HER TO THE MAN. "AT LAST!" THE MAN EXCLAIMED. "THIS ONE IS BONE FROM MY BONE, AND FLESH FROM MY FLESH! SHE WILL BE CALLED 'WOMAN,' BECAUSE SHE WAS TAKEN FROM 'MAN.'" GENESIS 2: 22-23, NLT

*Like a phoenix rising
she rose in slow motion
with the earth
reluctant to release her
pungent with its musky scent
soft and molded
resembling earth
with its mountains
and its valleys
crests and peaks
she rose
silently
hesitantly
gaining her footing
steadying herself
on long slim legs
that were yet unsure
of standing...
she rose and stood
breathing in the air
God had breathed into her
feeling her soul
unfold its wings within her...
the early dusk reflected
highlights of deep amber
red and golden brown
upon her skin
as the earth
from which
she had been formed
damp and moist
still clung insistently to her limbs
she rose
she stood she waited...
waited until he arose
this man
this setting
from which
she had been taken*

*even now
she felt the phantom remains
of other ribs encircling her
making her feel safe
as she awaited her discovery
...bone of his bone
flesh of his flesh
yet a separate entity
she breathed in harmony with him
feeling his pulse
hearing his heartbeat in her head
she was one with him
though outside of him
and when he awoke he knew
instinctively
profoundly
and definitely knew
that this was woman
a mirror of himself
the extension of his own arms
and so
he wrapped himself around her
tucking her beneath his heart
to keep her warm
and the two became one
balancing the weight
of life between them
and in the face of every tempest
she arose
in his strength
which had become hers
and hers his
she arose to redefine him daily
as a glorious testament
of all that was beautiful
all that was pure
and all that was good*

MICHELLEHAMMOND.COM |

*she arose
to embrace the origin
of who she was
who she would always be
woman
taken from man
from the earth
the signature of God
completing the sentence
that man had begun
bringing him to life
carrying the breath
of His spirit within her...
the glory of her man
the covering of her children
the giver of life
she could not be contained
for she bore all things
within herself
and in this capacity
she arose to give
as only
a woman can give
for it is a gift to the world
this creation
called woman...*

"Man is the head,
woman is the neck,
where ever the neck turns,
the head turns."
---African Proverb

"The power is in
the knowing..." --- MMH

Who told you that you were naked?" This is where it all began. The question that opened the door to the little lie that became an even bigger fabrication over the course of time. Who told you to be ashamed of who you are, woman? Who told you that womanhood has no worth? Who told you that the device God put in place to protect woman was evidence that she was unworthy of being acknowledged for her priceless value? Who told you that embracing your femininity was a losing proposition? Who told you that it's a man's world? A world where women should just take a backseat and accept their second-class citizenship in life? Certainly, these words never came from God's lips. And if God didn't say them, they have no grounds to stand up in court.

God did not design a man's world. God's design for the world was man and woman working together in peaceful harmony, building one another up and promoting each other to good works—namely our God-given assignments on the earth—that others would observe the fruits of our lives and give glory to God. Being a feminine woman is not synonymous with being a weak woman.

> "We women lost it when we failed to recognize our own unique power. Instead we got locked into a power struggle that never existed from God's vantage point."

Femininity has gotten a bad rap in recent decades. Femininity is not casting coy looks out from behind a fan. It is not wearing little lace gloves or swooning in the face of the slightest indiscretion. It is an inner quality that emanates from a woman who knows her calling and her value.

Feminine women are strong women because their influence is deeply felt. This influence gets beneath the surface because it is invited in. It is invited in because it is attractive and nonthreatening. It is nonthreatening because it doesn't seek to intimidate. You see, the feminine woman knows who she is and celebrates being all woman. She lets who she is naturally do all the work for her. Men fall all over themselves for that woman. And those women are happy, stress-free women. - **THE POWER OF BEING A WOMAN**

MICHELLEHAMMOND.COM

BACK TO BASICS

It is important that you know and tap into your most powerful gifts. They may not feel like gifts to you because they are so inherently a part of who you are. You are a natural when it comes to being influential. When you speak people listen. They don't just listen, they hear and obey! There is something about you that garners trust. Trust is a powerful weapon that is birthed out of nurturing.

Women are natural nurturers. Nations have risen and fallen based on the influence of a woman. I find it interesting that many of the cities and countries who fared the best during the Covid-19 pandemic were all led by women.

Our sexuality is a weapon we possess that has been the basis of wars being fought. The strongest of men have been seduced into weakness. And let us not overlook our capacity to reproduce life. Every person on the face of the earth had to pass through the womb of a woman including the Son of God--Jesus Himself! Are you feeling powerful yet?!

And lastly, the Word of God states that the woman is the glory of a man. A man's power is measured, not only by the type of woman he is aligned with, but by her state of being -- physically, mentally and emotionally. Could this be why God refuses to answer the prayers of men who don't take care of their wives properly?

God views women as valuable assets. The architects and finishers of the work He has purposed to complete before the beginning of time. Know that you are a critical part of God's great plan for society, your community, country and the world.

LET'S PRAY

Dear Heavenly Father, help me to see my femininity as a powerful force to be reckoned with. Help me to embrace my strengths and submit my weaknesses to you. Renew my mind to see myself and all that you have deposited in me through your eyes. Help me to live every day in the knowledge and understanding of my purpose. Heighten my sensitivity to the needs of those around me and let me be a vessel you use to produce life in others. In Jesus' name. Amen.

WWW.MICHELLEHAMMOND.COM

PONDER THIS

1. What misconceptions have you had concerning femininity in the past?

2. How can your femininity be an asset to help you accomplish your purpose?

3. Write out the definition of femininity. How will you utilize these traits?

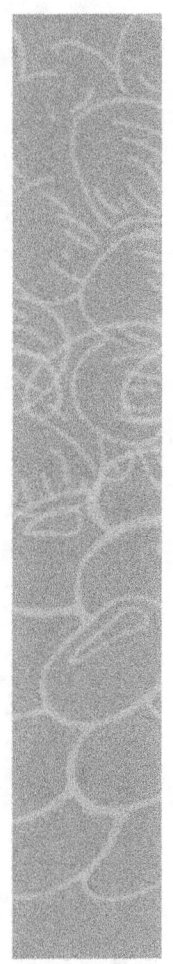

MICHELLEHAMMOND.COM |

TAKING THE LEAD

CHAPTER THREE

TAKING THE LEAD

NO ONE FROM THE EAST OR THE WEST OR FROM THE DESERT CAN EXALT THEMSELVES. IT IS GOD WHO JUDGES:
HE BRINGS ONE DOWN, HE EXALTS ANOTHER. — PSALM 75:6,7 NIV

*Wisdom spread her skirts
and sat beneath the tree
tucking prudence and discretion
beneath her feet
she flung insight
around her shoulders
to ward off the chill
of foolishness
and waited
for those who were willing to listen
to come the invitation had been voiced
that all who chose
the way of life should come
come and drink
of what she served
she waited
not insisting
not vaunting herself
on unwelcoming ears
for she knew that time
would tell the fulfillment of her words
and so she waited
basking in the light she had been given
allowing it to keep her secure
in all she knew
and when she spoke
her words were not wasted
they fell on the
fertile ground of thirsty hearts
that came craving refreshment
diamonds were given to only those
who recognized their value
for wisdom did not waste the gifts of God
on the undiscerning
saving them from stumbling
on self-imposed offenses
for wisdom knew that
timing was everything...*

TAKING THE LEAD

The common belief —and in great part it's a reality—is that in light of the times and most of our personal circumstances, "a woman's got to do what a woman's got to do" to survive. This is all part and parcel of what the sin factor delivers to our door. We must be careful, however, not to blame God for what is a natural consequence of man's bad choices. I use the word "man" in the collective sense. The bad choice that we make is submitting to the enemy's trick of utilizing masculine tactics in the marketplace. – THE POWER OF BEING A WOMAN

> **WHEN WE LOSE OURSELVES AS WOMEN AND BEGIN FORCING OURSELVES TO DEVELOP MUSCLES WE'RE NOT DESIGNED TO HAVE, OUR INTERNAL AND RELATIONAL SYSTEM SUFFERS.**
>
> --THE POWER OF BEING A WOMAN

TAKING THE LEAD

There have been many theological arguments over women in leadership, but I believe we must remain clear on the bottom line. Though man was first on earth, he was not alone. Woman was inside of man waiting for the appropriate time to be presented to him by God Himself. She was specifically chosen and molded with a very specific skill set that would help man function at his optimum level. Whether married or single, every woman is a conduit for a man's excellence. That being said, God will elevate women when men abdicate their rightful role and responsibilities.

In order to help a leader, you must be a leader in your own right. A suitable helpmeet is one who has matched, or superior, skill of the one they are assisting. They add to their partner and do not subtract! When we see women in leadership in the Word of God, we see women who advanced the course of their homes, communities and yes, even nations! God knew from the beginning women would be critical in His kingdom plan. You should never apologize or be a shrinking violet in circles that call on your leadership abilities. Speak with confidence and deal with others in grace.

A woman in leadership must remain cognizant that there is an order that must be maintained in order to be effective. Deborah, judge of Israel, mastered this. She did not take away from the men she led or make them feel "less than." She partnered with them. People in general will never resent instruction or assistance if they feel valued by their leader. It is the delicate dance of being firm and nurturing that only a woman can convey in her own way that brings unity and cooperation to any environment she inhabits. Remember, you were made for this!

LET'S PRAY

Dear Heavenly Father, help me to lead as you intended. Give me a heart of servanthood that makes others feel valued and willing to follow my instructions. Give me the discernment and sensitivity to those you have place in my charge. Grant me the wisdom to lead with grace in a way that reflects your character to all. Help me to effectively accomplish the assignment you have given me in a way that pleases you and blesses others, in Jesus' name. Amen.

PONDER THIS

1. What is your leadership style? Is it effective?

2. How is the "superwoman" syndrome hurting women?

3. How can you lead effectively without losing who you are in the process? Why is this important?

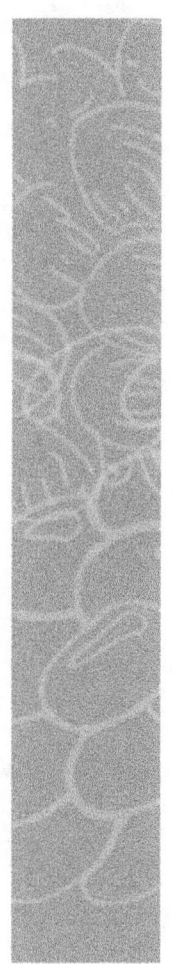

'BOUT BIRTHIN' BABIES

michellehammond.com | © 2020 THE POWER OF BEING A WOMAN

CHAPTER FOUR

'BOUT BIRTHIN' BABIES

ADAM NAMED HIS WIFE EVE, BECAUSE SHE WOULD BECOME THE MOTHER OF ALL THE LIVING.--
GENESIS 3:20 NIV

She suckled the child
against her breast
reveling in the warmth of this
her reward from heaven
a tiny innocent
so trusting
even now clinging to her
for its sustenance
it was not just milk
that she gave during
this maternal ritual
it was an impartation
of her spirit
of her heart
of her very soul
the key to their destinies
being released in the breaths
between her prayers
and the fluttering
of this infant's heartbeat...
yes, more than a child had been born
purpose had been born
born to a specific end
that would be revealed with time
so even as the babe clung to her
she clung to it
needing its nearness
as much as it needed her
both reveling in the closeness of the other
the quiet exchange of love
that needed no sound to express
its devotion
they drank in
the warmth of one another
lulling them both
into a place of rest
and quiet expectation
for miraculous tomorrows...

and within their inner beings
they inexplicably knew
they would always
be there for one another
the mother
and her child
the child
and its mother
inseparable
for they had breathed
the same air
shared
the same heartbeat
fed from the same source
of nourishment
from the beginning
their lives were
unexplainably intertwined
this was a bond that could
not be severed...
even if one attempted
to deny its existence
the bond would remain
an invisible cord
growing tighter
in times of crisis of sadness
of transition of loneliness...
of fear and questions...
growing tighter, yes
but never being severed
for their lives were
forever bound
inside of one another
this mother and child...

As we study the mothers of the Bible, the ordained calling of every mother becomes crystal-clear. Mothers are purveyors of life, created to give it, nurture it, protect it, and release it at the appropriate time to fulfill the purposes of God. I would dare to say that the role of a mother is so intensely powerful that the destinies of nations lie in her hands.

In essence, before any of us existed, God's plan existed. According to His foreknowledge of our personal dispositions, He was able to know which tasks to designate to whom in order to effectively carry out His purpose. We—you and I—are merely the clothes wrapped around the various purposes of God. You are here on purpose! And no matter how you feel right now, you do have a purpose.

It is a mother who is usually most spiritually attuned to the possibilities within her child. And she can nurture them like no other, gently planting seeds in that child's spirit and watering them with motherly encouragement as the years go by until one day, they bear precious fruit.

There is no such thing as being "just a mother" because motherhood is a precious assignment from God. It has its season. And in that season, enjoy the identity of being a Mother. Capitalized on purpose. Because God chose you on purpose for such a time as this. -- THE POWER OF BEING A WOMAN

'BOUT BIRTHIN' BABIES

I am just a mother" or "I am just a housewife" should never be spoken. There is no such thing as "just" when it comes to any facet of the myriad of duties and functions that women perform. Each is a sorely needed component that keeps the world turning and life running smoothly. Perhaps this is why the spirit of this world seeks to devalue and compromise what women are all about in the mind of God.

There is something about a mother. First of all, no one can land on planet earth without the life-giving capacity of a woman. It is that same woman who locates the strengths and gifts within her children and nurtures them to maturity and excellence. Any famous athlete or adult who has excelled at what they do inevitably gives the credit to their mother or a great woman teacher who told them they could "do it.

Though it may seem like a thankless task at times, your view of "getting" to raise children as opposed to "having" to raise children will make all the difference in your approach to your tasks and your joy level. Whether your efforts are obviously appreciated or not is not the issue. The bottom line is God trusted you and entrusted into your care what was most precious to Him to steward and raise to be an excellent member of His kingdom! That bears overwhelming weight and responsibility. Yet, the rewards are even greater. Motherhood is not delegated solely to those who bear biological children.

There are many women who have had children but are not mothers. The spirit of motherhood is resident in all who feel compelled to nurture those seeking love and direction from children to adults.

'BOUT BIRTHIN' BABIES (CON'T)

As a matter of fact, the Word says that those who have no husband will have more "children" than those that are married by virtue of the fact they have more of themselves to give to those in need. Single or married, know that you are a valuable part of Gods plan and your efforts have been recorded in His book for later renumeration past the compensation you will receive on earth. Embrace the high honor of motherhood and work it! This is where your greatest fulfillment can be realized.

LET'S PRAY

Dear Heavenly Father, thank You for the gift of motherhood. Help me to tap into your vision for my child (children) natural and spiritual. Help me to remain faithful to the assignment of raising godly offspring. Guide and direct me on how to do this best. Reveal the hidden things I may overlook that will be critical to their development. Help me to be a source of inspiration that points them to you and solidifies their godly heritage. Help me to also be aware of those you assign to me to nurture that may not be my natural children. Let the spirit of motherhood be evident in me to those who need it, in Jesus Name. Amen

WWW.MICHELLEHAMMOND.COM

PONDER THIS

1. Describe your mothering style. What are the positives/negatives?

2. What inner attitudes do you need to adjust in order to be more effective? Why?

3. What is your goal when it comes to your children? How will you facilitate this?

IT'S A SISTER THING

MICHELLEHAMMOND.COM | © 2020 THE POWER OF BEING A WOMAN

CHAPTER FIVE

IT'S A SISTER THING

... SO NOW YOU MUST SHOW SINCERE LOVE TO EACH OTHER AS BROTHERS AND SISTERS. LOVE EACH OTHER DEEPLY WITH ALL YOUR HEART. -- 1 PETER 1:22, NLT

Little pudgy fingers
full of wonder
pressed against unfamiliar lips
to see if her miniature visitor too
was warm
fingers equally inquisitive
and full of questions
reached back
reaching out
to entwine themselves
in locks of hair not her own
to see...oh, just to see
such is the way of babes
bearing no preconceived notions
no learned cautions as yet
they simply trust
and embrace
their first mutual giggle
becoming a covenant
a covenant to friendship
and sisterhood
and as the years struggled
to keep up with their height
their blossoming
their unfolding
into young women
the seasons changed as subtly
as the revelation
of who they were came to light
in the lines
reflected in their mirrors
these two women
who shared everything
from lollipops
to lipstick
now found that men
were more precious than toys

*and lines of permissible intimacy
were silently drawn
in the dawning
of the understanding
that some things
just couldn't be shared...
pain, yes
laughter, yes
discouragement, yes
an outfit, yes
men?...no!
absolutely not!
and the bridge was damaged
leaving gutters and trenches
that made friendship harder to cross
sisterhood more difficult to reach
and trust
woman to woman
an elusive treasure
and two little girls
now dressed in women's clothing
longed for a time they once knew
when they shared
and shared alike
when there were
no secrets between them
for they were all told under the covers
after bedtime stories
and goodnight kisses
when they were
closer than close
tighter than tight
thicker than blood
true blue friends
and sisters...*

This is a special feminine treasure—the ability of women to learn from one another. When women take the time to nourish one another and exchange their gifts, the fruit that comes from those lives is rich! When a group of women gathers to pray or to comfort a friend who is going through trial or heartbreak, the atmosphere is charged with power and healing. When women laugh together, cry together, or simply hold one another when there are no more words to say, it is an inexpressible wonder.

How much is missed when we refuse to be open to those around us, based on presumptuous assessments of one another. Our time and energy could be put to much better use. We should be busy helping one another prepare to receive blessings, helping one another look the best we can look and exchanging sound advice and encouragement. We will reap what we sow. What you make happen for others, God will make happen for you. As we purpose to build up another sister to help her step into the fullness of all that awaits her, we will reap our own reward. – THE POWER OF BEING A WOMAN

"This is my prayer for all women, that they will find the beauty in one another and reconcile their differences. Then and only then will we be able to erase the misconceptions of men and win them by our blameless example."

MICHELLEHAMMOND.COM |

IT'S A SISTAH THING

As I have travelled the globe many have asked me the same resounding question. "How do you find good friends?" Frankly this has always astounded me! I have been blessed to have a host of long-term amazing friends who have weathered the storms of life with me through thick and thin. From romantic loss, to financial challenges, health crises, family drama, spiritual seasons... they have been there through the good, the bad, and the oh so ugly. Still I chose not to have convenient amnesia of a different time in my life where my friendships were not so secure. I prayed and asked God to put enduring and quality relationships into my life. He was faithful to answer on one condition... that I would be the friend I wanted others to be for me. That mingled with a healthy dose of discernment on who qualified for the heart investment solidified me being surrounded by love and sound counsel over the years.

For those who struggle with their biological sisters the same holds true. Due to the issues that may create your family dynamic this can prove to be trying at times, yet with focus and determination the treasure of true sisterhood can rise to the surface. So dig deep and do the work it takes for your relationship to bear sweet and precious fruit.

Woman to woman relationships can be rich and fulfilling on several levels. Everyone needs a support system where your circle of influence champions you through trials and weighs in on decisions that are critical to your wellbeing. Everyone needs a sounding board that will speak the truth in love supported by non-judgmental objectivity and sound wisdom. True friends and sisters provide this. Women celebrating women also does one important thing—it influences the way men treat us. As we stand as a united force together, they get the signal loud and clear that respect must be applied in their approach. Remember others will only value us when we value ourselves.

LET'S PRAY

Dear Heavenly Father, help me to love and celebrate my sisters and women friends. Open my eyes to see them as you do. Make me a conduit of your love. Help me to always have a listening ear that hears past the surface to their true need. Strengthen my heart to love purely and without suspicion. Make me secure enough in my own identity so that I can celebrate them freely and without envy. Most of all help me to champion them to be all that you created them to be, in Jesus' name. Amen.

MICHELLEHAMMOND.COM

PONDER THIS

1. What have been your issues with other women in your life?

2. What insecurities do you have when you compare yourself to others? What beliefs do you need to replace?

3. In what ways can you be a blessing to your women friends? To your sisters?

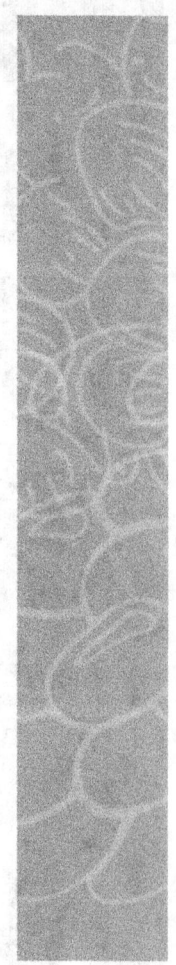

HOW TO BUILD YOUR HOUSE

MICHELLEHAMMOND.COM | © 2020 THE POWER OF BEING A WOMAN

CHAPTER SIX

HOW TO BUILD YOUR HOUSE

A WISE WOMAN MAKES HER HOME WHAT IT SHOULD BE, BUT THE HOME OF A FOOLISH WOMAN IS DESTROYED BY HER OWN ACTIONS.
PROVERBS 14:1 ERV

She opened the windows
allowing the Son
to fill the room
filling his world with light
this man
to which she said "I do"
with promises of to have
and to hold
for richer
or poorer
in sickness
and in health
till death do us part
amen
took in his surroundings
as she
the reflection of love
in his eyes
parted curtains of contentment
allowing a breeze of inspiration
to cool his brow...
an oasis
yes
that's what this home was
an oasis
a place of refreshment
and healing
from all the outside world inflicted
as she greeted him
with tender embraces
and adoration
serving him encouragement
and solace
piping hot and delicious
followed with a thick coating of
soothing
"you-can-make-it
because-I'm-here-for-you" sauce

her hand traced
creative patterns
on his shoulders
chasing away worry
and tension
while the scent of her
caused him
to have pleasant amnesia
about the cares of the day
home
was not only
where his heart was
it was where
his treasure abode
growing more precious
as the
years went by
sparkling in her eyes
as she viewed her handiwork
and the delight he took in it...
this miniature world
that belonged
to them alone...
yes, he was home...

As a wife, or a godly woman, the man in your life should feel that his heart, his secrets, and his emotions are safe with you. You should be the one to contribute to regulating his emotions and decisions, cooling him down when he's hot under the collar, and fanning the flame to stir up his passion for God, his ambitions, and his home.

You should be his haven of consistency, the one who is always there, the one he can always count on. He knows what to expect from you because your character is so sound. He should not come home every day to find a different woman who he can't figure out living in his house. He should have access to your heart, your softness, your reassurances, and your counsel all the time, and vice versa. You should be his oasis. He should be refreshed in your presence. And because of your good example, he wants to be the best he can be for you.

God is the greatest artist of all. No two snowflakes are the same. No two women are the same. No two men are the same. We are each unique, bearing our own set of individual needs and idiosyncrasies. Small wonder Paul said this whole marriage thing was a mystery. Imagine—two people walking as one in spite of it all. That is a divine mystery. That is why wisdom, godly wisdom, is required. "Wisdom has built her house; she has hewn out its seven pillars" (Proverbs 9:1 NIV). – THE POWER OF BEING A WOMAN

"Nothing affects a man as deeply as an encounter with a woman who has womanly qualities."

HOW TO BUILD YOUR HOUSE

One of my favorite songs highlights clearly that a house is just a house until a woman makes it a home. Hmm, what does that look like? Ikea and other outlets that provide reasonably priced furnishings have proven that one no longer needs to go to massive expense to surround themselves in beauty. However, it's important to note that the physical dimension of a home is only one element.

The spiritual atmosphere of a home sets the foundation for how you and others function in your personal world and beyond. One of warmth, love and order can make even the most basic and sparsely furnished habitation an oasis.

I have fond memories of living in Chicago. Every weekend my house was filled with the smells of delicious dishes and countless friends eating, laughing and solving the worlds problems. When I moved to Ghana many went into mourning wondering where they would gather. It gave me pleasure to have an open-door policy where anyone could stop by at any given moment for a respite from their individual storms. I recall my mother's home was the same. She had a reputation for being an amazing chef and baker. Our home was always spotless and inviting and everyone was always welcome to come by for a snack, meal and good conversation. It wasn't just the food. It was the atmosphere. Warm, welcoming and loving. A place that bred peace and security. That's right, home begins with you.

Who you are sets the stage for how your home will function and how it will feel to others. It's important to note that your physical house will be a reflection of your spiritual house. What lurks within your heart and your mind will manifest in your home. Bitterness and unforgiveness can create a cold environment while love and laughter create warmth that can be contagious to all who enter. The atmosphere in your home can breed love or division. Resilience or brokenness. So, nurture your heart and nurture your hearth, they work together to contain the life you want to live and share with others.

MICHELLEHAMMOND.COM

LET'S PRAY

Dear Heavenly Father, I give my home back to you and ask you to make it yours to be used for your purpose and your glory in my life as well as others. Let your presence always be evident to anyone who enters. I pray that my home would always be a respite and oasis. I pray that your peace and joy would reign in my heart as well as my home and be contagious to all that visit or abide within its walls. In Jesus' name. Amen.

WWW.MICHELLEHAMMOND.COM

PONDER THIS

1. Describe the atmosphere of your home. What would you like it to be like?

2. How can you make your home a sanctuary for others?

3. How can God be glorified in your home life? How can that be a blessing to others

THE STRENGTH OF VULNERABILITY

MICHELLEHAMMOND.COM | © 2020 THE POWER OF BEING A WOMAN

CHAPTER SEVEN

THE STRENGTH OF VULNERABILITY

IN EVERY RELATIONSHIP, EACH OF YOU MUST WRAP AROUND YOURSELF THE APRON OF A HUMBLE SERVANT. BECAUSE: GOD RESISTS YOU WHEN YOU ARE PROUD BUT MULTIPLIES GRACE AND FAVOR WHEN YOU ARE HUMBLE.
1 PETER 5:5, TPT

She called him Lord
and crowned him
with her graciousness
following beside
shielded by his protective arms
she basked in his shadow
all the while being his sun
her rays
bathing him in assurances
of greatness and esteem
whispering wisdoms in his ear
he did not reject
as she dressed him
in success before his peers...
and as her love
surrounded his heart
warding off the enemy
he did battle for her
covering that most precious to him
for she was his glory
his treasure
his pearl of great price
she stooped
he stooped even lower
not willing to lose sight of her eyes
eyes that said so much
without
saying anything at all
yet they gave him peace
in the middle of a storm
they made him see reason
when his own vision
was clouded with rage
they lit the way
illuminating his path
with sound direction
all the while
still calling him Lord

the pressure of gentle hands
pushed him onward
toward
the fulfillment of his destiny
soothing tired shoulders
stroking away worry
silencing the child
awakening the man within
as only she could
still calling him Lord
she held his world
steady in her hands
she filled his empty spaces
she repaired the breaches
in his spirit
and made him whole again...
she was his sanctuary
his food
his light
his queen
and still
she called him Lord...

TAKING THE LEAD

Submission is a command to everyone, men and women alike. Until we see submission as God's instruction to become vulnerable enough to receive, we will fail to recognize that submission is an invitation to be blessed.

Submission calls for you to be open to direction, emptying yourself of all your own ideas on the subject to make room for other possibilities. The next step is to close the door to your house behind you. After all, this submission thing is personal. It is between you, God, and your authority, whether that be your mate or your employer. It's not an open forum for everyone else to throw in their two cents worth. Submission will be easier for you if it is a private affair.
– THE POWER OF BEING A WOMAN

> "YOU CANNOT BE FEMININE IN THIS WORLD UNLESS YOU COMPLETELY UNDERSTAND HOW COVERED BY GOD YOU ARE. THEN YOU WILL NO LONGER REACT TO MEN, BUT RESPOND TO HIS VOICE."
>
> --THE POWER OF BEING A WOMAN

THE STRENGTH OF VULNERABILITY

Your attitude toward submission will color how successful you become in creating harmony in your relationships on all levels. When we see submission as yet another power move in our personal arsenal, we will embrace the opportunity to exercise our will to become a team player with those we have been assigned to whether single or married. Submission is an aggressive decision to walk in cooperation with someone. Whether that person is a spouse, boss, other authority figure doesn't matter, the principle applies across the board. We are all called to submit to one another as we recognize one another's strengths that can actually be to our benefit when they are embraced. Ego can distract us from the goal of winning at life or specific situations and rob us of the synergy needed to achieve the desired end result.

Sometimes you may know and have all you need to get the task done, however, because no one person can work in solitude, cooperation still needs to be achieved. Immediate success doesn't guarantee long term investment in what you want if no one else feels as they were a part of it. Others need to feel significantly a part of what you are doing. Submitting one to the other gives everyone a chance to play to their strengths and bring balance to the situation. It is cooperative checks and balances.

Simply speaking it is being a cooperative team member. In sports if the players spent all their time arguing over their positions and who got to run with the ball no one would win the game. Clearly defined positions decided upon based on the strengths of the players positions them for achieving victory. The same holds true with our relationships.

When we trust God to have the last say on our behalf we can surrender ground and firm stances on occasion, resting in the fact that it costs nothing to walk with open hands, while it may cost us everything to clench our fists and refuse to let go. The bottom lines. Submission puts us in the position to be blessed.

LET'S PRAY

Dear Heavenly Father, help me to remember that you are the one that is ultimately in control. Help me not to get stuck on what my eyes see or trust in the arm of flesh. Neither let me be so intimidated by others that I fail to see you at work in my life. Let your Sovereignty reign over all the decisions of men as I yield myself to your Lordship, In Jesus' name. Amen.

PONDER THIS

1. On a scale of 1-10 how would you rate yourself in the area of submission? Why?

2. What are your issues or fears concerning submission? What do we have trouble believing when it comes to submission?

3. In what ways can you practice trusting God more in your interactions with those in authority?

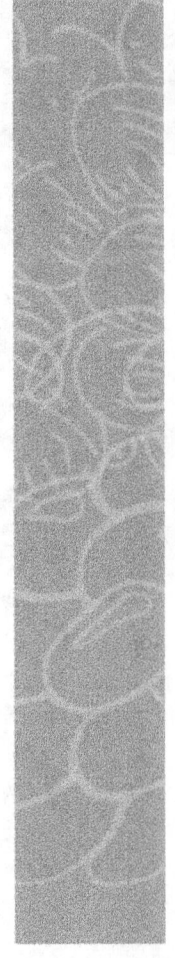

THE POWER OF INFLUENCE

CHAPTER EIGHT

THE POWER OF INFLUENCE

THE TOOLS OF OUR TRADE AREN'T FOR MARKETING OR MANIPULATION, BUT THEY ARE FOR DEMOLISHING THAT ENTIRE MASSIVELY CORRUPT CULTURE. WE USE OUR POWERFUL GOD-TOOLS FOR SMASHING WARPED PHILOSOPHIES, TEARING DOWN BARRIERS ERECTED AGAINST THE TRUTH OF GOD, FITTING EVERY LOOSE THOUGHT AND EMOTION AND IMPULSE INTO THE STRUCTURE OF LIFE SHAPED BY CHRIST.
2 CORINTHIANS 10: 3-5 MSG

*She spun her web
carefully
methodically
artistically
entrapping his mind
watching him
flail in indecision
pulled between his own instincts
and her suggestions
he tossed
amidst the silky threads that grew tighter
with every inner protest
and she watching from afar
gazed at her creation
trusting that he would see
the wisdom of her words soon enough
and just
as she thought it time
to move in and claim her prizes
her foot
became caught in her own snare
crying out for help
she realized too late
the help she sought
was also entrapped
rendered useless by her own hands
gazing at one another
across the distance of their predicament
they watched one another
die separate deaths
slowly
painfully
amidst misunderstandings
and a million regrets
he
for not being strong enough
to keep her from her own ruin*

*she
for not letting go of the reins
and grasping his hands instead
his hands
that now seemed
further away than ever
constrained
by her own determinations
losing the power they once had...
feeling her own strength dissipating
as she watched
the color drain from his fingertips
she realized all too late
that webs of manipulation
though beautiful in the making
were the most deceptive of all
their delicate lattice work
quickly transforming
into iron prisons
that bound both
"victor" and victim
the chasm of betrayal
too broad to afford them
the comfort
of one another's solace
as they quietly died inside
too tired to fight
too ashamed
of their own participation
in this most shameful demise
they closed their eyes
and dreamed of better days
as she concluded
that webs
were best left
to the work of spiders...*

Influence is overlooked because we are credit-mongers by nature. If we could just get over the need to claim the credit for everything that takes place, we would be able to achieve more than we ever dreamed.

If we could stop arguing over titles, we would see our wishes fulfilled and reap appropriate recompense and appreciation. When we free people to make their own choice to acknowledge us, it releases them to render praise Manipulation is likened to witchcraft, and God will never bless it because manipulation is an attempt to control through soulish means someone or something over which you don't have authority.

Manipulation strikes at the heart of man through intimidation or seduction, thus coercing subjects to respond according to your desire and against their will. This is where true femininity emerges as a clear victor. It triumphs over the barriers of misunderstanding. It disarms the hard of heart. It gently leads to a better way. It repairs the breach between those who have and those who are wanting.

God has given us the incredible power to convert men! Only a submitted woman can influence a man, or any type of authority, for that matter. The goal is willing cooperation. Going along begrudgingly does not build loyalty, but submission lowers the resistance to sound instruction and paves the way for a profitable exchange between the two parties involved.
- THE POWER OF BEING A WOMAN

"The gift of influence is the invisible power that women overlook."

THE POWER OF INFLUENCE

Being able to draw the line between your personal efforts in the flesh and allowing the projection of your spirit to inspire people to do the right thing can make all the difference in the world. Influence, like understanding, equips others to make choices by the strength of their own will. What other people decide they stand by.

What you decide for others has a fifty/fifty change of being sustainable. No one likes to feel coerced or manipulated. This will always lead to resentment and defection. This is why influence is more powerful than authority. Authority makes the person ordered to do something say, "I have to..." while the person who has been influenced says "I get to ..." They are fully invested because they feel they made the decision!

One of the most powerful gifts a woman possesses is her influence. Her powers of persuasion lie in her ability to help others see reason while nurturing them to a healthy place of understanding and cooperation. Women see things differently. I always say they are the color to a man's black and white. They fill in the blanks and put meat on the bones of a skeletal idea. They see the nuances and are able to make sense of the abstract. As they share their vision the eyes of others are open as well to see and embrace the possibilities they've been shown.

There is an art to it that rests in our femininity. No need to push or intimidate. Simply being you, rooted and grounded in truth with grace is enough.

LET'S PRAY

Dear Heavenly Father, I realize that when I trust you completely I don't feel the need to exercise powers of persuasion. Forgive me for the times I don't trust you enough and take matters into my own hands by bending others to my will instead of allowing them to surrender to yours. Help me to release matters into your hands and trust you to fulfill my desire, in Jesus' name. Amen.

WWW.MICHELLEHAMMOND.COM

PONDER THIS

1. What makes you doubt your capacity to influence others?

2. What is manipulation? How does it differ from influence?

3. What do you default to when things don't look as if they are going your way? What do you need to do in those instances?

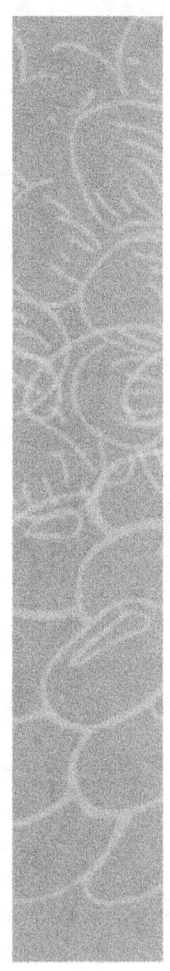

THE POWER OF INFLUENCE

CHAPTER NINE

GOING OVER HIS HEAD

AND OUT OF YOUR REVERENCE FOR CHRIST BE SUPPORTIVE OF EACH OTHER IN LOVE.
EPHESIANS 5:21 TPT

*She watched the glass
now empty
badly in need of a refill
her arms hung heavily by her sides
too weary from her constant revisiting of a task
she longed for him to do
he too waited
accustomed to her frequent attendance
he saw no need to break a familiar pattern
though he knew it was his duty
to refresh her
to fill her
she had done so well
refreshing herself
he now had no memory
of how to go about the task
and he wondered why
her eyes were so angry
though her speech did not give her away
the distance he felt from her body
when he reached to caress her
left unanswered questions in his mind
that he dared not utter
afraid of the responsibility
her answer might require on his part
and so
he waited
waited for her to refill the glass
but instead she just stood there
with her arms dangling
like leaden appendages
looking up toward the heavens
lips moving silently
pouring out her soul
tears streaming down
until they overflowed
the brim of the glass*

and as she reached for it
the unthinkable occurred
the glass tipped over
spilling its contents
rolling
rolling
rolling out of her reach
landing at his feet
and she still standing
not moving except
to see if her prayers had been answered
watched him bend to pick it up
staring
as if at a foreign object
finally a glint of recognition
lighting his face
he revisited his initial call
filling it with himself
he gave her to drink
and she partook
of his offering gratefully
still looking toward heaven
and then into his eyes
now filling with understanding
as the anger left hers
making room for softness in her gaze
as her arms regained their strength
no longer exhausted
from carrying both their loads
with one arm unfettered
she was now free
to embrace him
truly her glass was full...

At the end of the day, your relationship with your mate is only as good as your relationship with God. As a man's wife, you are called to assist him in the fulfillment of his purpose. Though we women are natural nurturers, we must submit this gift to God for His guidance on how and when to utilize it.

Ask yourself how much of your assistance to a man is fueled by the fear that if you don't make yourself indispensable to him, he'll no longer need you or want you. This is sin. Codependency, enabling—all of these are merely catch phrases to mask what one is really doing, which is stepping over the boundaries of the original assignment and infringing on God's job. God does not need your help.

So, woman, be free to be a woman, fearfully and wonderfully made, releasing your struggles into the hands of the Lord and the one He has put into your life to shoulder the load. And let that man be a man, even if it kills you to watch. - THE POWER OF BEING A WOMAN

"God wants us to delight in the way in which we were made and not step over the boundaries He so lovingly laid out for our protection and fulfillment. This is the feminine mandate."

MICHELLEHAMMOND.COM

GOING OVER HIS HEAD

Being able to draw the line between your personal efforts in the flesh and allowing the projection of your spirit to inspire people to do the right thing can make all the difference in the world.

Influence, like understanding, equips others to make choices by the strength of their own will. What other people decide they stand by. What you decide for others has a fifty/fifty change of being sustainable. No one likes to feel coerced or manipulated. This will always lead to resentment and defection. This is why influence is more powerful than authority.

Authority makes the person ordered to do something say, "I have to..." while the person who has been influenced says "I get to ..." They are fully invested because they feel they made the decision! One of the most powerful gifts a woman possesses is her influence. Her powers of persuasion lie in her ability to help others see reason while nurturing them to a healthy place of understanding and cooperation.

Women see things differently. I always say they are the color to a man's black and white. They fill in the blanks and put meat on the bones of a skeletal idea. They see the nuances and are able to make sense of the abstract. As they share their vision the eyes of others are open as well to see and embrace the possibilities they've been shown. There is an art to it that rests in our femininity. No need to push or intimidate. Simply being you, rooted and grounded in truth with grace is enough.

LET'S PRAY

Dear Heavenly Father, Forgive me for the times when I take matters into my own hands. I struggle to remember that you are God and I am not at times. I realize that others have to do things at their own pace. Help me to be as patient with others as you are with me. I release _____ back into your hands and trust you to work in them as you work in me. Help me to stay in my lane knowing you have all things in your control, in Jesus' name. Amen.

PONDER THIS

1. How do your expectations of others control your response to them not lining up with what you want?

2. What steps do you usually take in order to get others to line up with your plans or desires? What causes you to try to rescue others?

3. What do you need to do in order to release others to rise or fall on their own merit?

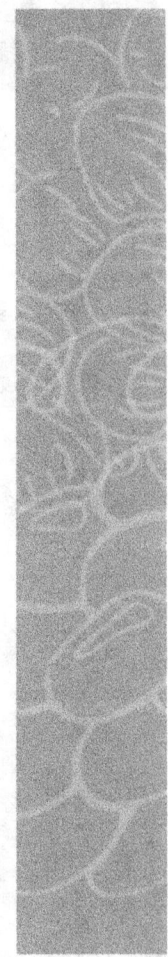

THE
POWER OF
INFLUENCE

MICHELLEHAMMOND.COM | © 2020 THE POWER OF BEING A WOMAN

CHAPTER TEN

AN OUNCE OF PRAISE

SO THEN MAKE IT YOUR TOP PRIORITY TO LIVE A LIFE OF PEACE WITH HARMONY IN YOUR RELATIONSHIPS, EAGERLY SEEING TO STRENGTHEN AND ENCOURAGE ONE ANOTHER.
ROMANS 14:19 TPT

My hero, she breathed
and he slayed yet another dragon
prompted by her praise
he arose to perform exploits
guided by the light of admiration in her eyes
Flexing spiritual muscles
as she waited for him to pray
he climbed
the stairway to heaven
and brought her back a rainbow
for her to wear
and as she told him
that he was her sun
he shone
as he had never shone before
and she in turn
opened her spirit
to drink in his rays
and warm her soul
in the fire of his eyes
drinking in his passion for her
she submitted herself to his covering
rejoicing in his love and care
feeling his arms tighten around her
she basked in his embrace
receiving all he chose to bestow
and he
responding to her need of him
dug deeper inside himself
searching for more to give
and as she poured out her adoration of him
he was quick to furnish her
with reasons for more honor

the strength of her love
the softness of her voice
the tenderness of her arms
were trophies
urging him to run with all his might
toward the finish line....
not counting the cost
the pain
the strain
a year seeming as a day
because the reward of her ardor
was so sweet
he would sell all
for one whispered confession
of how her heart moved
in his presence
for one glance from her
was all it took
to make his world stand still
for her
he lived
for her approval
he strove
for her touch
he breathed
it was for her
that he had his very being
for the absence of her adulation
was darkness to him
for she
who crowned him king
was his crowning glory...

Praise is as much for you as it is for the other person. Praise is an opportunity to rehearse the good in the other person. It is your way of reminding yourself why you are blessed to have this person in your life. It releases you from harboring past hurts or slipping into bitterness. It releases you to be joyful and releases the one who has been praised to cheerfully give to you.

As you struggle to walk in a life of purity, I encourage you to learn how to worship God. Be creative. Begin by creating an atmosphere for intimacy between you and the Lord. Then turn your attention toward the Lover of your soul. Begin to rehearse and thank Him for His goodness to you.

As your praise of Him escalates to the place of adoration, whether in word or song, you will ascend to another place of pouring yourself out before Him. As He meets you in this place, you will experience the deepest kind of satisfaction.
- THE POWER OF BEING A WOMAN

"Most of the time we as women give when we shouldn't, enabling men to be wimps, or we withhold when we should give, crippling the man from rising up and taking his place."

MICHELLEHAMMOND.COM |

AN OUNCE OF PRAISE

I recall a woman asking her husband one day, "Why don't you ever tell me I look nice?" To which he replied, "No news is good news!" While he expected her to know she looked nice unless told otherwise, his wife craved words of appreciation and admiration from him.

Depending on the environment you were raised in praise can be easy or difficult for you to give. Yet every person craves praise, appreciation and honor. It is in the depth of our fiber. It is validation and affirmation that we are okay, great, in fact. It is the stamp of our significance. It defines and motivates us to do even greater exploits. Small wonder some associate a lack of praise with a lack of love.

Even God desires praise as appreciation for all He has done for us. How much more those of us who are not as sure of our value as He is. It has been said that man represents the mind of God. In the mind of a man respect or honor equals love. They thrive on the honor the woman in their life renders to them. It becomes the impetus for them to accomplish even greater things. Ladies there is power in your praise. Men fall in love with you based on how they feel when they are with you. Respect not only draws a man to you; it makes him stay and be his best for you.

As women walking together, we also should give praise to other women where it is due. Being free to celebrate other women speaks of your own confidence and knowledge of what you have to offer. Withholding praise can be seen as an act of insecurity. When we can celebrate the achievements, looks and abilities of others it is proof of our own self-esteem and liberty. Giving praise is a step toward freedom and you release the attention from yourself to celebrate someone else and there is a place of complete joy in this once simple act.

LET'S PRAY

Dear Heavenly Father, let my worship of you extend to every area of my life. Make me a vessel of encouragement and affirmation to others. Help me not to allow envy or covetousness to make me withhold praise from others. Empower me to walk in gratitude and celebrate others freely, knowing that you are no respecter of persons. Help me to praise you and others from a pure heart, in Jesus' name. Amen.

WWW.MICHELLEHAMMOND.COM

PONDER THIS

1. How do you feel when others praise you and recognize your accomplishments?

2. What is the root of your struggle to praise others at times?

3. Why is praising others important? Why is praise so powerful?

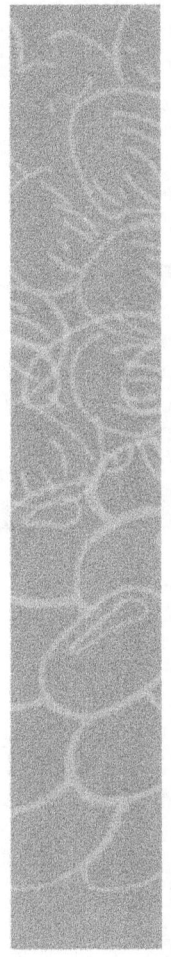

THE REWARD OF VIRTUE

CHAPTER ELEVEN

THE REWARD OF VIRTUE

WHO CAN FIND A TRULY EXCELLENT WOMAN? ONE WHO IS SUPERIOR IN ALL THAT SHE IS AND ALL THAT SHE DOES? HER WORTH FAR EXCEEDS THAT OF RUBIES AND EXPENSIVE JEWELRY.
PROVERBS 31:10 THE VOICE

He watched her from afar off
savoring her special brand of poetry
etched in every step she took
full of grace
vibrating with strength
a reed in the wind
bowing down
but always rising again
there was something about her...
he took her in
as she extended her arms
willowy and gentle
possessing secret power
not obvious to the undiscerning eye
her hands wiped
brows fevered with fear and trepidation
and healed them
her touch
as cool as her comforting words
soothed those uncertain
and gave sight to the blind
she moved soundlessly through confusion
leaving peace in her wake
while those before her
were warmed by her eyes
and the tenderness of her smile
yet strangely moved
even changed
by her appearing
unexplainable as it were
she left no one the same
so profound
was her influence
and though many
could not put their finger
on the exact word
that rearranged their hearts
they were sure of the source
it was her
something about her

for long before she was announced
her presence was known
it was felt
the air changed
her virtue saturated
the atmosphere
and brought rest
to tongues too busy
hands too weary
minds too troubled
it was her
something about her
not heralded but recognized
drawing like a magnet
all those thirsty for refreshing
her spirit gave them drink
and far more times than she knew
her closeness was enough
to set the captive free
to release those with severed wings
to take flight
and as she laughed in delight
they soared upon the music of her exultation
until they reached their destination
returning to roost
in the cool of her shadow
until she urged them on again
and as they rose
they carried her with them
tucking her in a safe place inside themselves
that they could revisit
time and time again
for in the end
the power they found to fly
was wrapped inside her prayers
coaxed forth by her faith
birthed by her...
there was something about her...

MICHELLEHAMMOND.COM |

To live your life according to what you, or those around you, think you should be doing is to live a life of frustration. You will always set the bar for yourself at some lofty level too high for you to reach. But as you seek God to find out His expectations of you from day to day, you will find yourself released to rejoice in exactly where you are. That is when you begin to sense the power of your position.

God plants us where we are needed. As we respond to His call and apply ourselves to what He has placed before us, we become a "force" to be reckoned with. We, too, must be saturated with our purpose as women. Only then will the serpent be rendered silent when we understand the value of our call.

Young's Literal Translation of the Bible says that when God confronted Eve about eating the fruit, she said that the serpent caused her to forget. She forgot who she was! She forgot what she was created for and went in search of prizes she could have received freely from God, if only she had done her job. Instead, she forfeited all that she had because she forgot her worth.
– THE POWER OF BEING A WOMAN

"The bottom line on this femininity thing? Women need men, women need one another, but most of all women need God. After all, we were really created for Him."

MICHELLEHAMMOND.COM |

THE REWARD OF VIRTUE

The secret to living a life of excellence is discerning your season and understanding the purpose of the season you are in. This is how you make an impact on your circle of influence and leave a lasting legacy long after your departure.

Understanding and focus breeds excellence that speaks well of you as well as the value of the gifts you utilize for the greater good of others. This comes out of knowing who you are. Having a sense of identity- your strengths your weaknesses and how to wield both in a way that is conducive to growth as well as thriving in spite of opposing conditions.

Being your authentic self--uncompromising in who you are and what you know keeps you on track to master the life you life with freedom and finesse. It also makes others take notice! It is in the midst of walking with freedom that virtue flows touching and engaging others.

This is the key to a life well lived-- rich in relationships, experiences and memories that leave positive deposits in the lives of all you encounter. Walking in truth--- your truth, God-breathed, God-inspired, God-directed. No need for hindsight. No regrets. Just lasting impressions of lives that were transformed by an encounter with you. Where everything about your life spoke of the reality of God and who we were created to be-- unique, richly feminine, powerful.

> "A woman who knows
> who she is,
> is a powerful tribute to femininity."

LET'S PRAY

Dear Heavenly Father, help me to appreciate and relish the season I'm in. Ground me in my relationship with you so that I can discern my purpose on a daily basis. Help me not to run ahead of you or lag behind. Strengthen me and give me the wisdom to master my present season in a way that pleases you and blesses others, in Jesus' name. Amen.

PONDER THIS

1. What season of life are you in? What is the purpose of your present season?

2. What things distract us from our present season and rob us of fulfillment?

3. What are some ways you can maintain balance and rejoice in where you are presently?

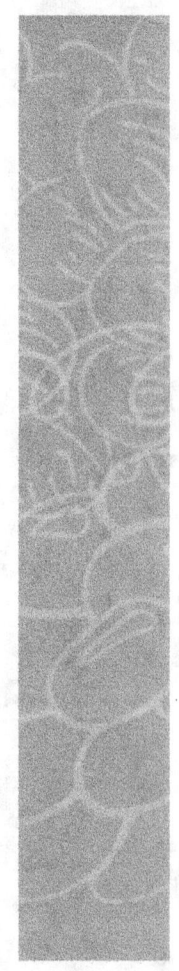

IN CONCLUSION

"Grace and peace be multiplied to you in the knowledge of God and of Jesus our Lord; seeing that His divine power has granted to us everything pertaining to life and godliness, through the true knowledge of Him who called us by His own glory and excellence.

For by these He has granted to us His precious and magnificent promises, in order that by them you might become partakers of the divine nature, having escaped the corruption that is in the world by lust.

Now for this very reason also, applying all diligence, in your faith supply moral excellence, and in your moral excellence, knowledge, and in your knowledge, self-control, and in your self-control, perseverance, and in your perseverance, godliness, and in your godliness, [sisterly] kindness, and in your [sisterly] kindness, love.

For if these qualities are yours and are increasing, they render you neither useless nor unfruitful in the true knowledge of our Lord Jesus Christ" (2 Peter 1:2-8 NASB).

To live your life according to what you, or those around you, think you should be doing is to live a life of frustration. You will always set the bar for yourself at some lofty level too high for you to reach. But as you seek God to find out His expectations of you from day to day, you will find yourself released to rejoice in exactly where you are. That is when you begin to sense the power of your position.

God plants us where we are needed. As we respond to His call and apply ourselves to what He has placed before us, we become a "force" to be reckoned with. We, too, must be saturated with our purpose as women. Only then will the serpent be rendered silent when we understand the value of our call.

Young's Literal Translation of the Bible says that when God confronted Eve about eating the fruit, she said that the serpent caused her to forget. She forgot who she was! She forgot what she was created for and went in search of prizes she could have received freely from God, if only she had done her job. Instead, she forfeited all that she had because she forgot her worth.
- THE POWER OF BEING A WOMAN

"The bottom line on this femininity thing? Women need men, women need one another, but most of all women need God. After all, we were really created for Him."

MICHELLEHAMMOND.COM |

MEET THE AUTHOR

MICHELLE MCKINNEY HAMMOND

Michelle McKinney Hammond is the president of MMH Ministries. She is the Best-selling Author of over 40 books, selling over 2 million copies worldwide. A popular International Speaker, Vocalist, Relationship Expert and Lifestyle Coach. She has spoken on major platforms ranging from T D Jakes' the Potter's House to the Crystal Cathedral and Walmart Corporation. A former Emmy Award-winning Cohost of the talk show Aspiring Women in the US, she also cohosted TCT's 3D Woman show. She has appeared on countless radio and television talk shows and been featured in magazines and newspapers in the US and abroad. She has appeared regularly as a Relationship Expert on major news channels in the US such as WGN News and Fox's "Fox and Friends" and continues to appear on major networks internationally. Michelle is a featured spokesperson with her own segment on Roma Downey and Mark Burnett's lightworkers.com and Light TV network. She is an accomplished Singer/Songwriter/Producer with 7 CDs to her credit. Michelle is also an Actress, appearing in several television series and movies in Ghana, West Africa. She is the visionary and Pastor of Relevance, a unique music ministry based in Ghana. She continues to travel, speak and perform internationally.

HAVE QUESTIONS?

+1-312-450-7175
info@michellehammond.com
www.michellehammond.com

 @MCKINNEYHAMMOND   MICHELLEMCKINNEYHAMMOND   MICHELLEHAMMOND.COM

More Encouraging Books

by

MICHELLE McKINNEY HAMMOND

∼

101 Ways to Get and Keep His Attention
The DIVA Principle®
How to Avoid the 10 Mistakes Single Women Make
How to Be Found by the Man You've Been Looking For
How to Be Happy Where You Are
How to Get Past Disappointment
How to Get the Best Out of Your Man
Right Attitudes for Right Living
A Sassy Girl's Guide to Loving God
Sassy, Single, and Satisfied
Sassy, Single, and Satisfied Devotional
Secrets of an Irresistible Woman
What to Do Until Love Finds You
Why Do I Say "Yes" When I Need to Say "No"?
A Woman's Gotta Do What a Woman's Gotta Do

DVD

How to Get Past Disappointment (180 min.)

∼

www.ingramcontent.com/pod-product-compliance
Lightning Source LLC
LaVergne TN
LVHW021410080426
835508LV00020B/2535